IMAGINE A TOWN

IMAGINE A TOWN

poems

Barbara Sabol

Sheila-Na-Gig Editions

Volume 4

Copyright © 2020 Barbara Sabol

Author photo: Janet Macoska
Cover art: *Maiden Lane*, acrylic on canvas, by Lizzi Aronhalt

ISBN: 9781732940666
Library of Congress Control Number: 2020931538

Published by Sheila-Na-Gig Editions
Russell, KY
www.sheilanagigblog.com

ALL RIGHTS RESERVED
Printed in the United States of America

To the places that claim us

Acknowledgments

Several of the poems in this collection first appeared in the chapbooks, *Original Ruse* (Accents Publishing) and *The Distance Between Blues* (Finishing Line Press). Grateful acknowledgment is also offered to the editors of the journals in which these poems originally appeared:

Blast Furnace Press: "Over-Easy at the All-Night Diner"
Blood Lotus: "Little Starling"
Comstock Review: "On Losing My Hearing" (awarded the Mary Jean Irion Poetry Prize)
Ekphrasis: "The Great Wave"
Evening Street Review: "Tending"
Literary Accents: "Dandelion Manifesto"
Monongahela Review: "Insomnia"
Pudding Magazine: "After Numerous Complaints of No Room of My Own"
Red Lion Square: "Convection Theories"
San Pedro River Review: "Landing"
Sheila-Na-Gig Online: "People Like That"
The Louisville Review: "After One of Those Summer Rains"
Tributaries, a Journal of Nature Writing: "Skipping Stones at the Oxbow"
Tupelo Press Poetry Project: "Poem with a First Line from a Fragment by Sappho"
Voices de la Luna: "Waking Without You"

Poems first appearing in anthologies:

Common Threads: 2017: "Hushed"
Common Threads: 2018: "Tea for One," (Ides of March poetry prize, Ohio Poetry Association)
Common Threads: 2019: "Ode to a Neighborhood Sidewalk"
& Grace: Selections from Lexington Poetry: "Red Bud"
Resurrection River: "The Cuyahoga Goes Unheeded"
The Ides of March: An Anthology of Ohio Poets: "Nyx"

Special thanks to Maggie Anderson for her generous and keen attention to this manuscript, and for helping to shepherd these poems into a book. To many friends for their support and valuable critique of the poems in this book, especially Nancy Chen Long and Jennifer Heald, my heartfelt gratitude. Deep appreciation to editor, Hayley Mitchell Haugen, for believing in this book. As always, gratitude to my mentors at Spalding University, for their indispensable guidance. I am indebted to the Ohio Arts Council for providing the resources to write. And, never least, to Tom, for everything.

Contents

I'm from a one-way bus ticket — 12

I.

At the Human Figure Exhibit — 16
La Turista — 17
Psalm with Summer Lawns — 18
Ode to a Neighborhood Sidewalk — 19
Ode to the Big Dipper — 20
Skipping Stones at the Oxbow — 21
The Mill Wright — 22
The Laughlintown Quarry — 24
In the City of Getting Lost — 25
The Descent — 26
Over-Easy at the All-Night Diner — 27
The Anything Will Help Cardboard Sign Blues — 28
Imagine a Town — 29
Late Snowfall — 30
The Great Wave — 31
Letter to a Wife Taken by the Waves — 32

II.

Hushed — 34
Convection Theories — 35
Witness — 36
The Magdalene at the Cleveland Museum of Art — 37
Afterglow at the Rust Belt Rebirth Exhibit — 38
Caleigh at St Michael's Parish — 39
Tending — 40
The Children's Home — 41
The Mermaids' Song — 42
The Bunny Bread Man — 43
Hula Girls — 44
Vertige — 45
On Losing My Hearing — 46

Husbandry	47
Dear Passerby,	48
Tea for One	50
People Like That	51
When the Blue-Hatted Muse Speaks	53
After Numerous Complaints of No Room of My Own	54
Waking Without You	55
Landing	56
Other People's Lives	57

III.

The Providence Bird	59
Dandelion Manifesto	60
After one of those summer rains	61
Red Bud	62
Once Upon a Town	63
Winter	64
Little Starling	65
Ode to the Salmon in the Grocer's Case	66
Insomnia	67
The Buck	68
Revelations *Redux*	69
The Cuyahoga Goes Unheeded	70
Vermis Equinox	71
The Spirit Fox	72
Nyx	73
Poem with a First Line from a Fragment by Sappho	74
Notes	76

For why do our thoughts turn to some gesture of a hand, the fall of a sleeve, some corner of a room on a particular anonymous afternoon, even when we are asleep, and even when we are so old that our thoughts have abandoned other business? What are all these fragments for, if not to be knit up finally?

—Marilynne Robinson
Housekeeping

I'm from a one-way bus ticket[1]

straight out of that town—factory whistle, iron works,
a dusty smoke stacked skyline. The overheated river's hiss
beneath the Allegheny ridges. Percussion of jake braking
down the mountain's grade.

I'm from rock: granite, limestone, the grainy quarry water
that floated us anywhere else under the blossoming stars.
I'm from watermarks outside the 12th floor of Swanks,
cipher for the city's resilience—rising from two
flooded centuries; citizens still treading water.

I'm from compound bow versus five-point buck; hunting season
trumped school. Back pocket Skoal halo. Red neck, blue collar,
pink collar, orange vest, my scratchy Catholic uniform.
Mass every morning. I'm from *O Sacred Head*—

we intoned the crown's piercing meanness, knelt before it
in clouds of frankincense. From the busy confessional—
a tether of venial sins: the cuss, stolen change, the hand
down there. Eve and her serpent; benign Blessed Mother.

I'm from nickel-a-prayer votives and the sanguine back of God
walking away from long unemployment lines—fathers, brothers, sons—
after the mill shut down. Labor unions fisted with dues.
I'm from too-proud-for-welfare, for food stamps.

I'm from green stamps, back yard gardens, sheets on the line,
the ham steak special at the Tick Tock Diner. From St. Casimir,
babushkas bent in prayer. From hand-rolled pirogue,
kielbasa reek, cold bottles of Pabst to cap long days.

I'm from the incline plane ascending from factory grind, up
to scrubbed suburbs then down again into the foundry's belly.
I'm from hand-stitched, home-cooked, nothing wasted.
Streetlight curfew, Archie comics, penny candy, four-square.

On frosted mornings the dairy truck's clink announced the *frisson*
of ice-cold whole milk. From the bakery van still-warm

white bread, Banana Flips; from canned goods stacked
against atomic fall-out. From the nimble illusion of safety.

I'm from Bob Prince's *swing and a miss,* from the hockey puck's slap
across War Memorial ice. JFK and Jesus, framed. I'm from whatever
is not polished, highfalutin, not some Emily's idea of etiquette.

I'm from the sparking trolley that ferried us into town (antique traction token
still in my jewelry box). At home on wheels, I jumped its grooved tracks,
motored past the city's strict boundaries. Their alarm at the threshold;
no backward glance.

I'm from a country of regret, of missing that gritty Shangri-La where
no one left and I returned as guest. Now an exit off the turnpike,
between Lake Erie and the coast. The place a vapor, thick as myrrh,
a recurring dream.

I

. . .What hasn't

been rent, divided, split? Broken
the days into nights, the night sky

 . . .into stars

—Dorianne Laux
"What's Broken"

At the Human Figure Exhibit

Bone to bone, her muscles cast
in half-tones, a delicate slackness
in the bulky architecture
of the aged reclined figure.

Wholly nude, save for a rolled turban
catching strands of her long, dry-brushed hair
whose loose coils slip their tether.

Across stippled paper her broad
dimpled backside to us as if
in a decisive roll away from our gaze.

My eye travels beyond the bend
of femur to knee, indolent truss of
what's cloistered, to the curve
of arm snug along her side, angling

at elbow into a nest of space
created by her body's arc, and I feel
the warmth of my mother's body
smudging those unholy shapes
in the darkness of my bedroom.

I lean into that sweet spin of oblivion
until my husband, ready to move on,
touches my shoulder.

La Turista
(a cento²)

Sometimes I am on a train
going to a strange city and you
are outside the window,
my beautiful capable daughter
far from home.

You were a *turista*. It is time
for loss to build its tower
in the yard where you are merely
a spectator now.

Think of your life as a bulky present—
stairway of shadows and lost dolls,
orchids in their hot glass houses,
bad luck and the black radish.

When the trees incline toward the grass,
arching with fullness, it's hard
to free your foot from that dreamy
earth-pull.

What a liar, the grave. Not one eyelash
stays underground. No one remembers
a soft wind off the stones of the dead.

Often I am permitted to return
to a meadow, consider the radiance,
a dream of the grass blowing.

The birds are there eating the rust
from their wings. Deep in my body
my green heart turns, and thinks of you.

Psalm with Summer Lawns
(a remix[3])

I cross the lawn in the valley of ranches—
gated, alarmed. Metal thorns wink
under the moon, its scattered light
skims the aqua water. Buzz of black flies, yet
I will fear no evil. In the darkness,
domestic motors throb like Latin drums,
tempo my steps down the path
of righteousness.

My hands cupped at the double glass:
a table prepared with gleanings and gleam.
Slight throats of designer dogs
adorned by diamond collars who
hiss at my face in the pane.
Their master lies, oblivious,
on feathered comfort in a room
full of Chippendale.

In the valley of abundance, they lack
nothing, conceal their shame
beneath joyful masks; forget that love
is a choice. I carry an iron rod,
keep my shadow to myself.
Anointed in the tawdry empire
of want, I will dwell in the house
of my enemies forever.

Ode to a Neighborhood Sidewalk

Squared off pathway from home to grocer,
you do not complain of weight, weather,
the wagon's ruckus. Neither do you mind
whose feet stroll or scamper, what wheels—
buggy, bike, skates—roll across
your purposeful surface. Fashioned to brace
every cadence, the suburban tumble and rush.

After decades of seasonal heaving and serration,
the city has anted up for fresh concrete, and now
your imprinted history—the hasty sneaker,
little handprints, your craftsman's WPA stamp
at the corner of Grant and 5th—will be archived
into a new patio or bridge. So, too, the neighbors' banter,
the sugar maple shadows blown across.

Ode to the Big Dipper

Slip with me, child, through the ragged
cyclone fence; the air here sparks.
Let's walk by the feeble coaster
where the wind turns shrill.
Even the Silver Rocket in orbit
over Chippewa Lake was eclipsed
by the Dipper's serpentine reach.

See how bindweed twines the latticed frame,
and dried thistle, iron weed scale the
corkscrew tracks that carried cars slow,
slow to the rise then
                    plunged—
    unhinged our grip to level earth.
Now un-done by oaks that split
the crosstie's nails and bolts; that
collapse the rickety shell of a thrill
into the abandoned park's understory.

O Dipper! Splintered bone heap
of reckless joy, wooden relic of amusement,
heart-in-the-throat conveyance, you are restored
in memory's gyres. I am transported
to ten, trespassed here at your crumble foot;
behemoth, splayed to the sky, to your
namesake constellation, given over
to a sad gravity, you bow to the ground
of our daring, our once shudder.

Skipping Stones at the Oxbow

We would pause at the broad bend
of the Cuyahoga, where river
abandons its plunge to the Great Lake,
maybe saying *rest, reconsider*.

Here the water flows across itself and draws
the land out into a spit, inviting walker
and tumbled stones to preserve a ritual
when little else holds—not the swell

of water or its rocky bed in spring.
In the light let down from the blue
suspension bridge, our crooked river
cut like a mirror edge through the gorge.

We knew better: the see-through larvae
were hatching in cleaner meanders, the king fisher
had deserted her lookout in the sycamore.
The city's industry bled *exit* into the runoff.

But we could forget all that when
painted trillium veined the trail, morning
sun tumbling through the naked canopy
down to where river clinches shore

and spreads. Here you encircled me,
pressed my arm into my side then,
hand over hand, taught me to execute
the perfect ricochet cross-current

clear to the other bank. My own stones
skip gingerly now: *one-two-three*
hops at most, before being swallowed up
by the rush and released downstream.

The Mill Wright

We dine atop the incline plane, suspended
above dormant industrial glory—the obsolete steel
mill, Bethlehem's iron sprawl—slumber-dragon shackled
to Allegheny Valley's blue-collar realm; smokestacks
hold their acrid breath. Against sunset, giraffe-neck cranes
bend on rusting joints in the silhouetted rigging.

Thirty-eight years my father labored, a journeyman rigger;
young and agile, he clambered scaffolds, suspended
like a trapeze artist. Balanced atop a latticed crane
he rode the platform's sway in the wind off the hills, steeled
himself against fear, against weary, against the stack
of woe on the counter. Love kept him there, shackled

to the notion of provision. My father accepted the shackle's
iron rub, its chafe against his soft nature—beneath the rigors
of winch and rope, torch and flame, his lot was stacked
with home-cooked comfort, arms 'round the neck. Suspended
between college and marriage, he had chosen to steal
my mother's affection with a steady wage, means to crane

the bricks, shingles, circuitry into place so they might crane
their dreams to children, to ribbons and tinsel, the gentle shackles
of family. As a girl, scant memory of him; the mill would steal
my father's daylight hours, his vigor. The Corporation, true rigger,
played grime-collar labor for its gain. Workers teetered in suspended
animation between blast furnace and bar. Hope, like dominoes, stacked

to tumble, another double all around. Next day's shrill whistle, stacks
exhaled the dragon's toxic breathing. Only the head of the crane's
main boom above gritted mist: my father, mid-air, suspended
over hot metal cars, coke oven—A Chagall in overalls, unshackled
to the engine room's black heart. His brand of faith, an invisible rigging,
secured him there—practiced hands, a common knot stronger than steel.

From the balcony we consider our hometown, far below a sky steel
gray as the old mill, monument to its rust belt heyday. Stacked
layer on decadent layer a chocolate torte for our desert; the rigging

of a certain privilege. Look! Leftovers wrapped in the shape of a crane.
A toast to our fathers, who kept this city humming. I am shackled
by the memory of him aged so young; by unspoken thanks suspended

in clouds over the mill. When the plant went under, elegant cranes
poised mid-swing. A final time-clock swipe; just like that, unshackled.
Single-file, workers passed the heavy gate, then into the air, suspended.

The Laughlintown Quarry

The boy I craved would tuck and coil off the rock face, glide
through the bottle green slur—his ribbed back tadpole-translucent;
nimble ghost fish, he barely ruffled the water as back and forth

across the pit's width he coasted, back and forth while
we wriggled, still wet, into cut-offs and tee's. In time,
others gathered, waiting for his seal-sleek form to surface.

The dark, broad basin of water had drawn us past
no trespassing to the high rock ledge of the limestone quarry
that sticky summer night.

A bunch of twitchy kids in a land-locked steel town, we caroused
the notion of a cool dip, a brush with what passed for love
at sixteen. The boys cannonballed into the mineral-thick water,

coaxed the girls to strip and swim from shore into
their submerged embrace. Our hoots and squeals shuddered
the piney quiet as quarry water glossed our limbs,
pale in the thinning light.

In the City of Getting Lost

I can't get reception, just waves
of white noise.

Street light burn pale as static.

Birds from my childhood startle
from beneath the bridge as I cross

and re-cross the narrow river slicing
this scratchily familiar city; the city

that is not my destination, but wants to be.

Its streets all return to each other, all uphill.
In my lightweight car I'm sure to tip backward.

Tilt and gravity twin bullies here.

Now I remember that dream—scaling
similar plumb inclines when my front wheels

lift. In a sweat, I'd awaken. But here I am,
dizzy, ascending, and in my tipping

recognize the row of fly-paper houses.
Nearly upside down now and there hangs

the War Memorial where we'd skate round
and round, insensitive to the chill,

the recurring scenery. Still I resist
the seductive, disembodied voice urging me

to make an immediate U-turn.

The Descent

Into the subterrain, my skate key.
No way but head-first down this gap
in the block's neat puzzle.

The neighborhood boys' grubby thumbs
notched my ankles as down the abyss
they lowered me; same chasm where

possum, raccoons would appear
when darkness curtained the street—always a shock,
the domed skulk, sewer to garden.

Lowered below my misfit existence
I squinted past the drain's perimeter into
a warren of wonders. Would its inhabitants—

mutants, mole people—welcome me in, kindred
in the outskirts of convention? The key's unnatural
brightness a promise of unlatch, enter.

The notion of brushing fingers with another
ambiguous being held my hand there longer, longer
as the crows gyred, raucous above and the kids' grip

began to slip—another inch now and
I scooped my key from its bed of muck, resigned
my small, altered self for the hoisting up.

Over-Easy at the All-Night Diner

I dump out the old brew and sizzle up the grill around dawn,
when the third shifters thin out and the day shift rolls in, then
I spot him; red stitching above his breast pocket reads, *Tom*.

In wrinkled coveralls, he leans on the counter and orders eggs
over hard; yolk hard as the August sun (bubbled like fresh tar
under his roller); leaves me his change and downs the dregs.

Most guys take theirs over-easy, they like for the yolk to ooze,
then sop it up with a slice of bread. Most still dreaming, eyes half-
open; maybe wishing the day was already over, but nobody says.

Bet he knocks off same time as me; I follow him home, in my head:
a tidy one-bedroom painted robin-egg blue; pictures on the walls.
We'd sleep in 'til whenever, and then I'd bring his eggs to the bed—

over-easy this time, spread jelly on his toast. Then he turns me once,
easy, over. I notice the color of his eyes. This is where it gets blurry—
we have nothing to say, or say nothing; either way, things get tense.

I'll keep an eye out for a guy with a sewn-on name, to float my theory
while I sizzle up the grill, scoop out fine-ground jo in no big hurry.

The Anything Will Help Cardboard Sign Blues
(a cento[4])

Unlatched, the swell of rush-hour sounds—
that sound like a prison door locking.
As red mist burns off the surface of the river,

the watchman dreams through his rounds:
the swale of afternoon, the sudden dip
of evening. Something has to hold you:

numbers, columns, a line of blue collars.
See, the world is busy and the world is quick.
Turbulent stasis on a blue ground.

Our spines promise to remember their shape
under the weight of light, a broken blue,
glinted off the forklift. The weight

of your days. All day, like this I short
my breath; hustle upstream. Hands turn the metal,
scrubbing, rinsing with a blue rag.

How souls are riddled with yearning;
we wake in the middle of a life, sweet blue light
spun out of nothingness.

You can howl your name into the wind
and it will blow it into dust, barely bigger
than a speck. Nothing is left but black and white.

So what could I do but wander the roads
drinking coffee from a paper cup,
go to bed with my feet dirty.

Imagine a Town

Gone grand *poof* some ghost towns
aren't inhabited even by ghosts
they don't stick around
for their own haunting
trusting the waterless wind
to bang the shutters no one
left to shudder, no one to slide
an arm around an imaginary back
practically feel the warmth grasp
an absent hand waltzing
around a darkened parlor.

Late Snowfall
March 17, 2011

over Sendai, its broken coastline, over
the orderly queues, waiting for a palm-
full of rice, an egg, a cup of clean water.
Between the swell of sea and grey-flanked
sky, the only refuge this warm-blooded
chain, each heart's voluntary knock.

Faces lift all at once as laden clouds
shake off their white spray of sorrow.

The Great Wave
after Katsushika Hokusai

Returning to Edo, our bekabune heavy
with sea bream and squid—skitter and slosh
in the wooden tubs. Fishing crew cradled
in the crook of wave, rocking us in
                              and out~
peka peka peka, waves slap the hull.

The sea crests overhead, presses its back
against the cobalt sky. Release the nori nets,
haul of seaweed. Grip the oars, dig into the rip-
muscled tide, flank of rising sea!

The great wave rears, front hooves paw the air.
Framed between flying mane and tail,
Mount Fuji. Its white-capped enchantment
suspends oars, fishermen, the whole spun world
in a circle of soundless air.

Letter to a Wife Taken by the Waves
Fukushima, 2011

Twice I returned to the coast, looking for the red coat
you wore that day, even though the air had been warming.
I prayed I would find you safe inside it. That you would walk
into my arms. Each time the great wave rebounded, chased
half of us back to the highlands; the other half it swallowed.
Muffled screams still wound my ears.

A week now since the tsunami's random bound to shore,
its last retreat. I have come to comb through our rubbled lives.
An iron pot strewn with seaweed, shards of a headboard, blue
glass pearl bead, ink-smeared pages from a tablet–your fine script.
A brown ceramic knob, sad as a cow's eye; no door, no rooms.
Ragged photos in the mud.

Intact somehow was your natto bowl; I inhaled the fragrance
of fermented beans and yams and fell to my knees in the dirt.
Its green crackle glaze a fine net around the bowl, the etched
galloping horse: muscled, fearless, unbroken. I traced its shape—
mane, kicking legs, wild tail—and smashed it against the ground.
I saw you then, dear wife, your face aglow, red coat sinking
below the horizon.

II

What separates self
from the flutter of longing?

—Mary Szybist
"Twelfth Night from the Willow Cabin"

Hushed
for Annie

Some days the blossoming sweet bay suggests
the Chesapeake, and her girlhood lifts like the call
of gulls laughing across wide water, this far
inland. On such days she is parched from the dry
scrabble of sounds—cluck and scratch of chickens
in the clay earth. Since the day her brain gasped
for oxygen, the blind weight of her tongue gropes
for sound—clapper swinging mid-air; no bell lip
to catch it. Scratch and cluck. Dust in the mouth.
When winter stars lodge in the evergreens, she chokes
on each point of *star*. Once she could have said *exquisite*,
and this would have been said so easily, a sigh of syllables.
She could have said *come outside, my love, look at the sky*,
and they might have stood watching light pulse
through the quilled branches, with no need
of speech; the perfect words roosting on her tongue.

Convection Theories

Before the storm, anything
but calm–wind catches
the private undersides of oak leaves,
holds them up to the elements,
and then with that first crack
of thunder I am running
to unplug appliances large and small,
checking ghost currents that might set us–
you, me, the dogs, the end tables–alight.

Last month a storm like this sent
a pin oak crashing right through
my neighbor's roof into the front and back
bedrooms. It was early evening, thank God,
and they were downstairs, just
finishing dinner.

Somehow the whole family managed
to walk out the front door, survey the wreckage
of their wooden house. Spared survivors,
they stood linked together on the sidewalk,
repeating to their unscathed neighbors,
How lucky we were, how blessed.

So quick, that spear of light, the heart-
splitting howl of opposites in motion.
Then the release of a cooling downburst.
Here we flip the switches back on. Breathe.
If only our inevitable fights could work like this—
wild whip of words, our tendernesses exposed,
then the generous abandon of rain.

Witness

Remember that summer night we drove
down to the cornfields of Holmes County?
We wanted to witness the fields lit
by a tentative mesh of starlight—fireflies
blinking above the harvested stalks.

We were so young, pulsing
with wonder ourselves, never
running out of words, enchanted
with how our minds synapsed in union.

What does it matter if you forgot
what you had for lunch today,
or those three ridiculous words
the doctor wanted you to recall?

What matters now is that you can picture
how the field was aglow with the flashing code
of fireflies, a full field of them, signaling back
and forth, a warble of light in the rural hum
of cows cudding, horses shifting their muscled weight
in the dim stalls, the stripped husks' dry *shurring*
in the breeze.

And remember how we felt about all this magic
as we sat on the bench seat of your green Plymouth,
the one with the push-button transmission.
Our first car.

You pulled me into a world radiant with wonder,
your arm around me, squeezing my shoulder,
a brief kiss, luminous, before the complex web of light
vanished into the expanding darkness.

The Magdalene at the Cleveland Museum of Art

Among the *Treasures of Heaven*—
the carved sarcophagi, mummified fingers
of martyrs, their last agonal gestures—
a tooth from Mary of Magdala, pearly incisor
laid on a pillow of crimson silk.

There is no statue of her to kneel before
in any Catholic church. No image
of her radiance on any devotional card.
Yet here, next to the splintered remnants
of St John's true cross, this vestige
from the mouth that discovered the artless lexis
of love with a man she believed could save her.

Enclosed in a rock crystal case, braced
by gilded silver and copper brighter
than the yellow maples outside the gallery,
this simple enameled relic may have fallen
from the skull of any ordinary woman
from any bygone age.

I needed to believe it truly was
from the Magdalene, patroness
of misplaced women, the only Mary
to whom I can pray.

Afterglow at the Rust Belt Rebirth Exhibit
    inspired by an industrial art lamp by Kevin Busta

Storm sky vessel of light
tamped into a zinc and steel edgeless—
bolt charge inside
a bruised summer cloud.
                      Switch

to that time on Lummi Island—
we found a row boat in scrub grass
pointed stern-first toward the Salish Sea.
Earth streaked, muted blue peel to the bone.

At home once in the swell and chop;
weathered now by harsh maritime—
persistent fog, sand and pebble wind-brush
against the hull.

Its body laden with splintered jute rope,
sun-bleached rock, oar-end of a paddle.

Weighted more lightly
by soft wave-froth,
cirrus wisp, sun angled
through a gull's wing.

The old boat held all the flimsy island light
we needed to see by.
                      Illuminated

anew on a restored scrap metal table,
this low-lit reclamation—
salt air sifted through the glow.

Caleigh at St Michael's Parish

He offered his hand to his aged mom
when the fiddler switched to a three-four meter.
One gentle spin 'round the parish hall.

Agile in his grasp, she swayed to the waltz;
walker aside, she danced unfettered.
He offered his hand to his aged mom.

The mood in the hall shook to a calm—
just fiddle, shuffle and lapping sea water.
One gentle spin 'round the parish hall.

In his arms *a-one-two-three* into some
much younger time, her limbs far fleeter.
He offered his hand to his aged mom.

The cut of his features, his smile, seemed a balm;
the son so resembled his father.
One gentle spin 'round the parish hall.

Then sat her back down to the room's soft applause.
O! To still have your mum, cried the caller.
He offered his hand to his aged mom.
One gentle spin 'round the parish hall.

Tending

The day was bright and busy
with graveside visitors
generous in the softness
of loss: an offering
to the distraught woman
digging in the dirt
with her hands.

Above-ground, my mother
would have *tsssked*
at my incompetence, arriving
with a box loud with marigolds,
a potted red geranium.
No trowel, no soil, no jug of water.

She might smile now
at my fumbled gesture
of love, my eternal tussle
with the simplest of things.

A supple wind passed once
through the vividness
rooting around her stone,
and I knelt back
on the scuffed earth above her,
finally able to cry.

The Children's Home

They spilled from the County Children's Home
like assorted candies from a glass jar, clutching
their props—wiffle ball, chalk stubs, skip rope—
then were dutifully scooped back up by dusk.

On summer days Frankie and I would study them
from the safety of our front porch; we hunched
above our ice cream cones, spinning tales: survivors
of a spy ring bust, train wreck, an avalanche.

Within our Irish Catholic clan
the hands of bountiful aunts folded us
into the brood—numerous, unremarkable
but always accounted for.

The orphans' fate was a rudeness greater
than our greatest loss: the missing Betsy doll,
the kitten caught beneath the tire—calamities
we couldn't imagine.

Our grade school brains were not prepared
for chance fortune, tart as home-made rhubarb sauce—
we savored the sticky drizzle and the delicious fiction
of being possessed.

The Mermaids' Song

Mr. P was my Latin instructor at Our Lady of Sorrows.
He tried to make the dead language relevant. How he loved Horace!
We made devil's ears behind his back. Or dozed. *Contrapasso*
for our irreverence.

Mr. P was our neighbor. He lived in the grey shuttered house
three doors down. Kept to himself, often wandered the streets
at dusk with his old yellow lab. Usually muttering; maybe
conjugating Latin verbs: *audĕo, audetis*.

He'd hike the collar up around his neck, even on summer nights.
Always dressed formally—never jeans and sneakers, never a cap
over his balding head, no matter how chilled the night air.
His students made fun of his shiny pate, his futile comb-over,
the *mysterium* of his bachelorhood.

If he happened to be on the porch, my father would call,
How you doing tonight, Al? Nice night for a walk.
Maybe I only imagined Mr. P's wince at the cheekily
familiar salutation, the nickname's distinctly blue-collar ring,
the invasion of his reverie. He would tip a pretend brim
and nod, *perfunctorium*, in his direction.

He was less awkward with me, but I was just a scrawny tomboy,
bucktoothed and disheveled. He tutored me in the classics,
and my grateful mother would serve him tea and cakes.
Pleased to have an educated man with whom she could discuss
Michelangelo. In the lamplight, I would catch him beholding her;
more than just looking. *Et vidi*.

The last time I saw Mr. P he was walking down the middle
of our street on a bright afternoon. Wore an untucked, striped shirt,
khakis rolled to the knee and flip flops! In his hand a half-eaten peach,
dripping juice. As I wondered, *What's gotten into Mr. P?* the sidewalk
and all the houses shook as if the earth had shifted off its axis.
Perago universi!

The Bunny Bread Man

We knew him by first name only, saying, *Thanks, Joe,*
when he set one loaf of white, one of rye, atop the milk box.
Trust back then was common as butter bread.

Joe was enlisted to fetch me to school when I missed the bus
days in a row: I longed to color alone in my room, comforted
by yeasty oven smells, the Electrolux whir.

He'd idle at the end of the drive, settle me on the back bench
of his aromatic van between columns of Snowballs
and cream-filled cupcakes.

One morning Joe changes his route, passes corners I don't recognize.
The school bell will be sounding, and now we're headed down
a gravel road. Joe whips around with a tight smile when I ask

where are we going, goes red in the face when I begin
to whimper, makes a hard, merciful U-turn when I stand,
wailing, lose my balance, land under a mound of confections.

Afterward, routinely early to the bus stop, not minding
the boisterous older kids, standing close to Miss Ellen,
the school secretary who couldn't drive

because of her glass eye, which was no longer scary.
At lunch I would peel the bread from my sandwich, toss it away
with gristle and spoiled bits of fruit.

Hula Girls

The clerk held out a black one-piece suit,
material thick and shiny as seal skin,
with a diagonal design meant to trick the eye.

She assured me it was fashionable, revealing
just a hint of thigh, white as twice-whipped
potatoes. But I chose the gaudiest of the bunch—

yolk yellow with red piping—daring to be visible
this maiden summer of my leisure years. The skirt wafts
above my waist, brazen manta flashing

like the Hula Girl hibiscus bushes Mother and I planted
each spring: we tamped the soil with vermiculite,
staining our fingers with creaturely smells of dark appetite,

and tasted bits of mica in our sleep. All summer,
I pinched out the stem tips so the showy flowers
with their ruby eyes could bloom continuously.

In my two-piece job, I bob into the current, toes curling
in the lake-bottom ooze. My hair silvers the water,
a flowering crown.

Vertige
Paris, 11/13/15[5]

> *There were bodies everywhere.*
> —Julien Pierce, witness.

> *He who contemplates the depth of Paris is seized*
> *with vertigo. Nothing is more fantastic. Nothing*
> *is more tragic. Nothing is more sublime.*
> —Victor Hugo

How odd, everyone said, the trees clinging to their color
this late into November.

A boon of pleasant. Of beauty.

The sassafras yellows deepened, lobes
palm-up to the Indian summer sun.
They glowed past dusk.

The maples' burnt orange bled into wing seeds
tempting the wind to spin them into air.

Yes, unseasonably warm. A wonder, everyone said.

The buckthorn's greens stayed longest; sprigs of berries
ripe into snow tricked the robins into staying
past ground freeze.

Plucky along the tree lawn, the trees bore their foliage
to the elements, dry tick and scrape of leaves
in the uncommon breeze.

We kept our sleeves rolled, slept with the windows open.

Our beech held open its broad, rusty parasol against the rain.
My neighbor and I often meet beneath it, talk about the world,
how it's changed, what we're fixing for supper.

Last night we stood breathing in the sweet decay.
Rain pocked the leaves overhead.
Awoke to a great unpredicted gust that shook the leaves—
a carpet of red—over the wet, black pavement.

On Losing My Hearing

The day begins absent the steady tick
of the kitchen clock imitating a thin rain
against the window, an under-the-skin
rhythm to the morning's choreography.

Absent the fricative's wash of *ocean, azure*;
sounds that vibrate in the elevated frequencies
of speech so that *shame* becomes *home*.

Summer, the *thwack* of a butcher knife
through the season's first melon, pitch
of a cricket's wing against toothed wing.
Its passion call lost in the night.

The train's moan through the small hours' darkness,
exact timbre of longing, curls a body into itself
soothed to hear its own sadness fading.

O minute trio, hammer-anvil-stirrup, always alert
for the familiars—clock, song, the lock's quick tumble—
stilled. The crinkle of this page turning, unheard.

Husbandry

Deer step out of the thinning woods nightly: hunger
makes them bold, almost tame. They head for his
gentleman's garden in the side yard; experimental
carrots and bib lettuce striking roots.

He bound the plot with spiked wire. Protection
from motley appetites invading our land. Cursing
with each sharp prick, he finished the useless fence
in one night, then mucked the knob with dirt and blood.

At dusk I watch as two does approach, their heads a soft angle
to the tentative morsels. They accept the snag and pull of wire
over muzzles, black gums drawing back as they work
the bitter husks of winter tomatoes.

I think the taste must be sweet to them, like living.
Let them feed. What harm? But he runs at them and they scatter
into thin suburban wilds. Mornings, a wasted breath
clings like dew to the backs of melons.

Furtive creatures with those eyes viscous black, quick, the deer
snort and stomp just inside the tree line through our broken sleep.
Would they settle for tufts of bunch grass, forsythia sprigs—
easily spared satisfactions—if we just let them in?

Dear Passerby,

Witness of the tragedy variations, you skim the internet
with your first coffee, hover a silk remove from the singe,
the siren—compass gone wild.

Scroll past misery-faced refugees, plastic-laced ebb tide,
another body count. Coffee gone luke and bitter.
Scroll now to things benign—the weather, Dear Abby.

Sure, it smarts but the faster you scroll, more like
a paper cut, cramp, an oblique ache and you can move on
while some bristled thing nests.

Today a news story attaches itself, common dust
you can't shake off. A woman driving home,
drinks with friends after work, maybe a hellish week,
maybe some kind of celebration, cheers all around.

Misjudged arc and distance where road abuts
the sidewalk's curve; there at the corner
she broke that spooning. Metal and glass.

Knocked an old man walking his dog,
both man and dog, that soft spring evening,
out of existence.

Here she is, pictured in a grey jumpsuit, posed against
a cinder block wall, bent forward as if some sharp force
just struck her between the shoulder blades.

Under the fluorescence, her features a pucker of horror.
She looks familiar and in some fleeting degree of separation
you and she might once have chatted at the market—how to
roast asparagus, keep mint from taking over the garden.

She could be you, be me—respectable, hard-working,
neighborly. Until now. Happy hour a bit too.

The air of stupid fortune acquires a taste, impossible
to rinse, and it hits you how a quick jerk of the wheel
can crack your long-coddled world where all that hatched
seemed well-formed, normal.

Tea for One

I take it at break to remain clear and civil.
I take it at cafés, gleaning the paper;
on the front porch, inspecting the neighbors.

I take it with whiskey, a thimble-full, at breakfast.
I take it at two, with crackers and butter.
At night alone in bed with a story.

Like a mean truth, I take it bitter, no sugar.
Like a tonic, I take it in lean swallows.
Like an old love, I take it weak.

With its garland of wood smoke, I take it grateful;
with its tang of familiar skin, I take it aching;
with its whistle and sting, its beads of sweat, I take it.

People Like That

Only when her brute dogs would escape
through the broken windows would we see her—
new age Medusa, turning our hearts to stone.

Voice at full-throttle, gut hung over the wrought
iron rail, she'd curse her hounds in lingo
that made mothers pull their children in from play.

She loaded her van and moved to Vegas, left the place
to the vagaries of suburban nature. Scum around our block,
a snub to civility, we said, yet were drawn

by the ammonia reek, the debris strewn
across raw floorboards. We cupped our hands
and peered in through spiked-out coronas

of glass in the half-moonlight, pressing
from every angle as if for a glimpse
of The Bearded Lady or Alligator Girl.

One sticky summer night we raided her riotous garden—
perennials swarmed the cement stoop, insinuated
their tendrils beneath the eaves.

Rhododendrons flamed the cedar shakes
and snap dragons whispered their blooming.

First one neighbor, balanced by two scrappy buckets;
soon others trickled down the walk, growing brazen
with wheelbarrows and shovels.

We uprooted fiddlehead ferns, white violets,
the tea rose bush. Whole shrubs.

Only the Japanese maple remained inviolate;
it held and released handfuls of light as we grunted
and dug on our knees in the dirt, marveling,

above the trowels' chafe, at what becomes
of people like that.

When the Blue-Hatted Muse Speaks

    Like middle-aged lust, inconvenient
and startling, the urge comes fierce.
Triggered by someone talking
about downing some Red Stripe
at a motel in Lodi or by a blue
pillbox hat in an old *Life*
photo (black and white, but I know
it's blue), complete with netting—
her painted lips mouthing something
I can almost make out.

    Another time by some falling-
down shed in a cornfield, County Road 27,
on a day so hot the cobs roast as they grow.

    Enough to send me, nymph-swift,
shoeless, to my desk, to listen
to what the blue-hatted woman
is whispering. She knows the taste
of Ohio sweet corn, dripping
butter, chased by an iced cold
bottle of beer.

    Backlit by flashing neon—*Vacancy*:
She insists *describe it, black on white,*
my inspired, vivid kiss.

After Numerous Complaints of No Room of My Own

My husband marked off the bounds of livable
basement space—2 x 2 furring studs of raw
blond wood—a frame ready for its inspiration.

He heaved unwieldy sheet after sheet of dry wall
down the narrow stairs, sanded, plastered, snugged them
between the beams, over bristly pink insulation,

conjuring private quarters—an island of comfort
within an expanse of grey cement. Until then I could imagine
nothing other than an ordinary, cob-webbed cellar

suitable for dank motors of cooling and heating,
sumps and pipes and whatnots—a domestic dungeon
I'd visit like a pampered survivalist.

Now a body might escape the overlit upstairs hubbub,
might sink at last into reverie in the polyphonic
underbelly house hum, the unruffled air; here, lit

by a hurricane lamp, at this mission desk. Side walls extend
from a clean white base, a horseshoe-shaped space
welcoming scribbler and scribe, welcoming me—
                                        lucky, lucky.

Waking Without You
for Tom

Even when I am lost in a strange city, foreign
road signs, no right turns, circling back, frantic,
I still register your gentle tumble into bed,
warm snug into the waiting space, and I breathe
deeper into a new dream.

Tonight, my hand traces your missing shape, and I count
every dark molecule of distance between me
and the hospital bed where you lie, attached by leads
and tubing to cold, metal monitors.

The wall behind you resembles some kind of
space ship cock pit; screens blip pressure, breath, beat,
rest, beat while my own heart lurches.

Now your side of the bed is an open crater,
sheets cold as this night's half-moon and you
as far away.

Landing

Surprised still by
his stockinged tread
up the stairs, soft
thud for a man
so large; the breadth
of his shoulders
seeming to span
every stair-width;
surprised, too, by
his gesture's sweet
weight—removing
his shoes in the
dark so as not
to awaken
me as I lie
listening to the
white oak boards creak,
as if the house
means to settle
deeper into
its heartwood, all
the way up the
stairs his foot fall
is lit by street-
light and prospect.

Other People's Lives

We wake to find ourselves
      in other people's bodies   older
           people housed   in crepe paper skin
who look back at us
      with weary eyes   swimming
           with memory   and now
we inhabit   someone else's house
      designed for limbs   tired
         of climbing   we know
a single story   that once   we
      were we   and all
         was simple
ascent   there is a bird
      at the feeder   I
         don't recognize
blue-breasted
     his constant
         treble song   life
is a con artist   steals
      your regular heart beat   un-
         ravels
your vigor
      beside the porch   a vine
         variegated   twining
           in the rain
I used to
     know its name

III

let me catch sight of you again going over the wall
and before the garden is extinct and woods are figures
guttering on a screen let my words find their own
places in the silence after the animals

—W.S. Merwin
"Vixen"

The Providence Bird

Before my walk, quiet domed the neighborhood.
Nothing but rain-weep through the gutters.
Then the clear ascending twitter of a prairie warbler,
rare here, in my garden.

One quick block from home: just
missed the swift cleft of chrome
metal-on-metal yowl
rubber reek and slam as
a black van somersaulted onto
a flare of poppies, suspended
a woman in the driver seat,
wild-eyed, swimming her arms
through the upside-down air.

I did not know the name of that sun-yellow bird
or recognize its charmed song. I had gone back in
to check my field guide; within moments,
located its name.

Dandelion Manifesto

We are the inexorable gold heads each with some hundreds bold
florets that pock the lawns with cadmium announcements We are
edible medicinal potable beautiful brilliant bringers of bees and
every spring the neighbor stretches his lank aging frame across
his front yard panning through the grass for order or evil then
leverages his special tool designed just for this against the moist
soil to yank our demon brass buttons He forages down to our roots'
tendrilling nerves His lips a tight tremor of syllables as he parts
lime green blades scours the ground in a passion of eradication
Our starry seed heads from one untended lawn will waft again
this season to his Accidental marriage of neglect and purpose
Gentle reminder that nothing in this world is perfect and that
                                                                    it is

After one of those summer rains

quick and hard odors of the district dogs lift
from blades of grass scented Braille
chronicles of dominance rolled newspaper
rabbits chased nearly caught juicy reports
my dogs read rapt slender muzzles pressed deep
in a curb-side patch though they've breathed in
many variations on these themes one never tires
of one's own history sensitive brutes I imagine
the part they linger over longest is of a fellow lost
a cautionary saga about the follies of freedom here
I don't tug saying *c'mon c'mon* each chapter matters
so they learn by heart which corner leads home except
now noses lift to a wet breeze streaming over hedge
and hoods of passing cars a fresh account that holds us
even longer out in the ordinary evening air

Red Bud

    Since that season of winter thunder
we expect our red bud will become
a collection of kindling—wizened trunk
home to flicker or nuthatch; like us,
inventing new ways to remain useful.

    Yet each April it spouts
unique pinks, its own fragile vigor,
despite that long-ago lightning
blazoned its gnarled body, setting the blush
aglow
        while
  small green hearts
appear from
           nowhere
                      and everywhere.

Once Upon a Town[6]

•

Even in the haze of phosphorus and sulfur,
the match factory workers could not have imagined
their town burned and flooded, and for Boston's thirst—
Grange Hall, the grist mill and tanyard leveled.
Prescott's apple orchards overwhelmed with water,
spilling from earthen dams as the broad bowl
of Swift River Valley filled and flowed, drowned
the industry of four towns.

•

Grey wolves still roam Quabbin Mountain, low-slung creatures
circling the quarry in what was Dana, mill town known
for soapstone footstools, double-bowl sinks. Only stone walls
and cellar holes of farmsteads left. Remnant roads lead
below water. Walking at dawn, I watched from behind the pines:
wolves crossed the ice to feast, a fresh-killed fawn—one
standing guard, one eating, in turns. The pair trotted off then,
drawing their shadows back into the woods.

•

The fog gives back the landscape in a gradual release
of the hilltop's bony prominences. Breadth of shoreline
shapes the water. The sky resumes its blue weight,
its high silence over steeples and shops. I row out, squinting
against the sun burning off the mist, as a veil would lift
from the face of a woman.

•

I row across water sleek as satinette, light tricking
oyster shell buttons across the surface. The quick hands
of factory women. At the near shore an apple nods
in the current, a Search-No-Farther: no, a fisherman's bobber.
And beneath the blue smoke that rises, flame-like,
the pattern shop, the dye house, the hall. In the white-petalled lilies,
a likeness.

Winter
Inspired by a fragment from Sappho

Winter is a country
that settles
in your limbs, stirs
the joints—mortar,
pestle—and your own
weather shivers
against the changes
as it takes up
residence
in the vintage bones.

If not winter,
it's your years
that hush the blood,
cooling
the snow-pebbled skin
as your own
paler season
seeps in,
by degrees,
with little fuss.

If winter, you take it
all in—what choice
but to absorb
the fading, green-
tinged light;
like absinthe, color
of forgetting, first
and last
color
of the world.

Little Starling

Craving nothing but air to ride, or a kind
kindred look, something she cannot name,
no one's darling squeals, launches down
the walk on the balls of her high tops, flapping
tucked-in arms like silly chicken wings and
chanting to the branches, alive with the song
of spring's nuisance iridescent puddles of oil
whose return is the illusion of having been gone.
Neighbors startle at the rattle from yellow
bills then again at the whistle from inside
the hood of her yellow slicker,
                        whoooeee, she mimics
the mimics, studies their purple-sheened dazzle,
shies at the whine of her odd mustard coach,
then quietly boards the gifted kids' bus.

Ode to the Salmon in the Grocer's Case

Displayed as specimen, head and all,
on a fine mesh of ice. A hint of your luster
under the fluorescence, laid out as you are,
arched as if mid-leap, in the grocer's glass case.
What rivermouth, this land-bound Midwest
town of thin tributaries and plowed earth?
Adapted to travel between salt water and fresh,
water to fire; no maker ever intended this
last unhallowed move—on view in the unbreathable,
your ray-finned splendor torqued over frost.

Insomnia

I am especially drawn by the produce—
green hues induce sleep at two in the morning
when the pastel breath of pears and iceberg
reminds me of what I cannot have.

Radishes incubate in the misted cooler.
Haunted by their night-light glow, so unlike
the eggplants that taunt: purple-black skin—bruise
shine—color behind my eyes when they close.
Sometimes old women who have slept enough
for one lifetime will share secrets
of detecting ripeness. One holds a cantaloupe
like it's growing from her solar plexus, presses
nose to stem, taps the orb then her chest,
twice: *mea culpa, mea culpa.*

I want to slice right into the orange meat;
never mind the placental mess or the night
manager. Imagine the taste—biting, bright—
white seeds catching in the throat, like first light.

The Buck

Consider the buck in the scalloped glade
of my neighbor's yard, statuary until
the breathing from his sueded ribcage.

Behold the buck, his rack two Y's
sheathed in velvet; delicate, ill-equipped
for skirmish, for claiming his place
in the order of things.

Pity him, drawn from hospitable woods
to this world of strategic thickets. Streetlights
blot stars surfacing over back yard pools.

Admire the moist orbits of his
brown gaze, how the tawny light slants
across muzzle and arched neck.

He might have stepped
from a *fleur-de-lis* tapestry into
this suburbia. The winged stag.

Regard his grandeur, how it summons
a lostness, and for a stretched moment
we stand at the lintel of adjoining worlds,
alert to the strangeness of each.

A quiver runs the length of my dogs' leashes.
We inhale unruly roses and lilies, the delicious
wildness in the grass.

Now follow his echoing clop, soft across the asphalt,
toward somewhere beyond the thoroughfare;
ghosted by twilight, the busy whiz of east/west traffic.

Revelations *Redux*
(a cento[7])

I can't tell anymore for whom I grieve,
my tongue feeling large for my mouth.

Pears in their boxes were golden
and full. Wheat berries
piled in metal bins. Now, ice
and its melt stream are strangers.

Birds are speeding overhead,
and the unmown field is foaming,
leaving a seed grave.

How do we love what is damaged?

Our days lacking much of anything
that can be named. I should fill them
with trees.

At night, strange apparitions and sounds
that I can never identify.

In that second when everyone senses
the lurch and spin to come, I believe
He is coming the way I believe
the rain will stop.

What now is the prairie sky
if not another relic, burning?

I hold it in my hand as long as possible.

What shall I do
with all this heartache?

The Cuyahoga Goes Unheeded[8]
circa 1969

My broad, muscled back manages
all manner of vessel—the heft
of barge or urn may float the spine
and curves of my body. Lavish in its flow
and brace. A solace, my constant rock.

Dyed a rust-brown, camouflage
for debris that swirls in the slick
that's become my skin, rinsed
not even by the abundant rain
in this city of steel skies.

Gulls with their saltwater bouquets
no longer swoop my cyanide depths,
bereft of bluegill and walleye.
Silence now above and below.

Inevitable, the errant spark—lightning,
careless match, a passing train.
Listen! The gods of fire and water
are gathering by the tracks.

Vermis Equinox

It's not air or escape
from saturated digs
so much as the impulse
toward creation that lures
the earthworm back above
ground—the flaccid grass slick
as a just-born, under
the last few shards of snow.
Worth risking the robin's
beak, the groundhog's grubby
clutch, is the writhe along
the length of its see-through
segments, each link purpose-
driven: one to burrow,
one to digest, and two
to ooze out a cocoon.
Either way, for breath or
love (blind to the difference)
they shimmy up, powered
by five minuscule hearts.
Each muscled ring a clause
dependent on the next:
God's first articulate
terrestrial sentence.

The Spirit Fox[9]

Well nourished, sharp-

      eyed, he returns
           from his shrine

in the eastern mountains
      to this flat kingdom
           of frost.

Our quiet street shaken
      by this wind-glossed copper smudge
           parting the gauze of January.

He jaunts past, devil-may-care
      in his black spats, gazes
           right through me

balanced by my shovel
      at the edge of the drive; grip
           on the handle loosening.

I watch until the black tips
      of each of his nine tails
           slip

behind the thin veil of snow.
      Agarwood, rice straw
           incense the brittle air.

Nyx[10]

The drenched air suddenly wing-shuffled—
the red wing's abrupt tumbling call. I realize
I've been listening for the blackbird's hark,

the familiar trill. Voice of an intimate, come back.
Turn and turn, search the grey landscape—quicken
to Nyx who cracks the dark void, marrying sky to earth.

The Lakota hear the red wing's cry as *Oh! That I might die!*
To die while the memory of push and crown, root, stalk,
thrum of sap into the tub, clenches in the chest.

The great swirl circles counterclockwise—milkweed
recast as seed in the waiting pod. On the brink of this
obsolete lock, I watch the sluggish water pulse with return—

toad rouses from the mud bank, black snake unribbons
from her suspended life, warms her blood below
on the crumbling pudding stone wall.

To die in the middle of miracles when the rusted wheel turns,
sluices the flow and sweeps me onto the thawing chest
of water, into the creaturely colors of the season.

Oh to be lifted off this lock into the weightless hands
of March wind, while the earth drinks in the sky's blue
and heaven swims green with river, river!

Poem with a First Line from a Fragment by Sappho

No more than the bird with piercing voice,
    this sweep of light across the grass, evening
        quickens. The wood thrush calls down
            the last plumes of violet, bruising the
                                          air

beneath—the familiar double-warbled cry. Though much
    is understood about the bending of light, passing
        through one medium (say, dimming day) to
            another of less velocity (say, a glass,
                                          water)

how is it the light, along with the bird and its sorrow song,
    bows, if you will, along some vector, an angling of x
        toward a denser y, so that what we perceive
            shifts as we look, slant as a fault in the
                                          earth.

Nothing truer than my palm curving the shape of your thirst
    and its quenching, as I carry a glass of tap water,
        brimming, out through the twilit yard, to where
            you sit aslant the darkening
                                          sky.

Everything, even the water in its amber tumbler, all
    its immaculate droplets intact, stills and is held by this
        tapering half-light, by the pitch of a half-recalled
            call, response; the glass, our hands
                                          vanishing

Notes

[1] Inspired by George Ella Lyon's poem "Where I'm From."

[2] Cento with lines from A.R. Ammons ("The City Limits,") Robert Duncan ("Often I Am Permitted to Return to a Meadow,") Steven Dunn ("Dismantling the House," "Juarez," "From the Garden,") Erica Funkhauser ("What a Liar," "Into the Blue Core,") Rochelle Hurt ("The Old Mill,") Phillip Levine ("Grandmothers in Heaven,") Sharon Olds ("The Winter after Your Death,") Ruth Stone ("Scars,") Ellen Bryant Voigt (from Messenger,) David Young ("Broken Field Running.")

[3] Remix from the lyrics of Joni Mitchell's "The Hissing of Summer Lawns" and Psalm 23

[4] Cento with lines from Graham Barnhart ("What Being in the Army Did,") Tiana Clark ("My Therapist Wants to Know about My Relationship to Work,") Henri Cole ("Middle Earth,") Billy Collins ("Morning,") Mark Doty ("Four Uncut Sunflowers; One Upside-down,") Edward Hirsh ("Second Story Warehouse," "Cotton Candy,") Dorianne Laux ("My Brother's Grave,") Phillip Levine ("Office Hours," "Ashes,") Alice Miller ("New Wings,") Sharon Olds ("The Winter After Your Death,") Mary Oliver ("Singapore,") Lucia Perillo ("Say This,") C.T. Salazar ("Poem with Three Names of God + a Promise to Myself,") Myrna Stone ("The Lost Boy," "Sonnet for Sarah,") Jane Wong ("Everything," "After Preparing the Altar, the Ghosts Feast Feverishly.")

[5] On November 13, 2015, a series of terrorist attacks were carried out in Paris, leaving 130 people dead and 494 others wounded. ISIS claimed responsibility.

[6] In 1938 the Swift River Valley in Western Massachusetts was flooded to create the Quabbin Reservoir, to satisfy Boston's growing demands for water. Four towns situated in that valley—Dana, Enfield, Greenwich, and Presco—were lost to the reservoir. Old roads leading to the towns still run to the water's edge.

[7] Cento with lines from Bruce Beasley ("Gnomic,") Harlan Bjornstad ("Profit/Loss Statement,") Chelsea Dingman ("Epistemology,") Joy Harjo ("Speaking Tree,") Tony Hoagland ("Game,") Gail Martin ("How I Will Feel When It Stops,") Sara Michas-Martin ("Middle Life,") Lynn Pattison ("Free Fall,") Jack Ridl ("Hardship in a Nice Place,") Omar Sakar ("Where I Am Not,") Ann Sexton ("Rowing,") Bianca Stone ("Hunter,") David Young ("Broken Field Running.")

[8] Cleveland's Cuyahoga River caught fire in June 1969 due to decades of industrial pollution—an environmental drama that helped engender the federal Clean Water Act of 1972.

[9] The nine-tailed celestial fox is an auspicious figure in Chinese mythology. Fox spirits have been worshipped in China since the Tang Dynasty. In the Way, a celestial fox is said to transcend yin and yang.

[10] In Greek mythology, Nyx is the Goddess of Night, born of Chaos and one of the first elemental gods. The black bird is a significant symbol in Greek and many Native American myths, serving as a messenger to the gods, and as a creator god who brings life to the world.

www.ingramcontent.com/pod-product-compliance
Lightning Source LLC
Chambersburg PA
CBHW071030080526
44587CB00015B/2560